THREE HOTELS

ALSO BY THE AUTHOR
The Substance of Fire and Other Plays

THREE HOTELS

PLAYS AND MONOLOGUES

JON ROBIN BAITZ

THEATRE COMMUNICATIONS GROUP

Three Hotels: Plays and Monologues is published by Theatre Communications Group, Inc.,
355 Lexington Ave., New York, NY 10017.

Baitz, Jon Robin, 1961–
Three hotels : plays and monologues / Jon Robin Baitz.—1st ed.
ISBN 1–55936–085–2
I. Title.
PS3552.A393T48 1994
812'.54—dc20
93-51492
CIP

Design and composition by The Sarabande Press
First Edition, May 1994

Contents

A Note from the Playwright

I think I first conceived of Three Hotels as an act of vengeance on my parents' behalf—this being the kind of hubris only children are capable of, and only when they believe, erroneously or not, that they have witnessed the humiliation of a mother and father.

Memory is everything to me. In an earlier play, I have a character say, "I live each day only so that I may have something to remember tomorrow." Sometimes I think that is the playwright's life (or this playwright's life). Fallible and dangerous as memory is, I do, however, quite clearly recall the phone ringing in my parents' small, somewhat charmingly cramped Beverly Hills apartment, and me picking up to hear my father say, "Well, Robbie, they finally did it. They let me go," and then a slight laugh of bitter relief.

As it transpired, my father, who had worked for the same company for thirty-some years and had risen amicably through the ranks, had been one of several vice presidents who were asked to "take an early retirement" that "Black Monday," as it came to be known in family mythology. When he retired, I think he became someone else, a man in what was only definable as "the second act" of his life. My mother was relieved that all the traveling, the secret battles for corporate survival, the hours and days lost in a cold sweat of work-fear, the failing health, the diminution of spirit—these would all finally end.

That is *not*, I hope, what *Three Hotels* is about. It simply served as the leaping-off point for what I now realize is an ongoing attempt to understand the unknowable nature of two people I have loved and wanted to protect ever since I was a child, and thereby to learn something about my own flawed and leaky little psychic bag of tricks.

I think what I write about is betrayal. Consider the story of the scorpion who encounters a water buffalo at a riverbank and implores the buffalo to ferry him to the other side. The water buffalo, reluctant at first, says, "You'll sting me; I know you," but the scorpion *swears on his life* his good intentions. Of course, halfway across, the buffalo feels the inevitable white-hot stab of the scorpion's sting and asks, wonderingly, "*Why?* Now you've killed us both!" To which the scorpion replies, as they go down for the third time, "I can't help it; it's my nature. . . ." This, to me, is maybe the only story there is, and one simply lives to see it proven or disproved (disproved more often than not, I think, I hope.)

Three Hotels is most assuredly *not* a play about my parents, but a rumination on betrayal of one's self, one's hopes; and finally, it is the fervent prayer that there be something in this wrecked world to salvage. I wrote it very quickly at a beach hotel much like the one described in Part Two—a hotel exactly like the kind of place I grew up in transit at. After seeing the play, people sometimes express the desire for an actual scene of dialogue, but at the Hoyles' hotel there is no talking. There is only a terrible, aching silence, which can only be bridged by the longing to feel that one is still human, even though there is little evidence left to support that wish.

All of the other pieces in the book (with the exception of "Recipe for One, or A Handbook for Travelers," written for a benefit at Circle Repertory Company) were written for Naked Angels, a theater company that has been a home to me in New York, and a place to work on a small scale between the more scarily public outings that are the playwright's lot. I am terribly grateful to have had such a place, and such friends as Fisher Stevens, Geoff Nauffts,

Patrick Breen, Ron Rifkin and Joe Mantello, Naked Angels all. I have been unspeakably lucky, I realize, to work as a playwright, and to be surrounded by so many people who happily have no place in the sorry fable of the water buffalo and the scorpion.

—Jon Robin Baitz
8 February 1994
New York City

THREE HOTELS

This play is dedicated to Joe Mantello,
who brought it and its author to life.

An earlier version of *Three Hotels*, produced by Public Television's *American Playhouse* in 1990, was directed by the author and won him a Humanitas Award.

Three Hotels was originally produced on the stage in July 1992 by New York Stage and Film Company in association with the Powerhouse Theater at Vassar College, under the author's direction. Later the same summer the play was produced by the Bay Street Theatre Festival in Sag Harbor, New York, under the direction of Joe Mantello.

Three Hotels was produced by Circle Repertory Company, New York City, Tanya Berezin, Artistic Producer, in March 1993. Joe Mantello directed the following cast:

Kenneth Hoyle. . . . . Ron Rifkin
Barbara Hoyle. . . . . Christine Lahti

Debra Monk took over the role of Barbara Hoyle in May.

CHARACTERS

Kenneth Hoyle
Barbara Hoyle

PLACE

Part One: The Halt & the Lame
Tangier, Morocco

Part Two: Be Careful
St. Thomas, Virgin Islands

Part Three: The Day of the Dead
Oaxaca, Mexico

THE HALT & THE LAME

TANGIER, MOROCCO

A hotel suite. An air of faded Edwardian quietude hangs heavy in the air. Kenneth Hoyle stands for a moment in thought. He has on a rather exquisite summer suit. There are manila files, papers, old copies of the London Financial Times, etc., scattered about the room.

HOYLE: The first thing I want to say is, this is an interesting market. This little corner of Africa here. And it's been a particularly bloody morning here in Morocco, let me tell you. Because one of the interesting things about this market is we lose more money here than anywhere else in the world. Which believe me, is saying a lot. Because we lose money everywhere.

So this entire morning has been about cutting away the deadwood, and when I say deadwood, think of a petrified forest, okay? Letting people go. That sort of thing. And gruesome work it is. I mean, to fly in and check into some hotel and tell people it's over is not exactly . . . a joyride.

Markets. At World Headquarters in Los Angeles, we have a sort of War Room. And there is a *map.* A lucite map of the world, upon which our competition appears as a sort of huge orange cancer encroaching. This is the same orange as the drink *Fanta* which is popular in my markets.

(Beat)

Third World Markets. (They like us to say "Developing Nations" which is slightly laughable given just how little development occurs.)

(He goes to drinks tray and takes his time mixing a martini)

I sometimes think that if we could color our product, which is powdered baby supplement, a powdered-milk formula, if we could just color our product *orange* like this drink Fanta, a fun color, appealing to the natives, we might increase our sales threefold overnight.

"Five'll get ya ten," I say at our meetings in the War Room, that if this baby formula were bright orange, fizzy and sweet, we'd knock 'em dead in Lagos. Gets a bit of a laugh out of Mulcahey and Kroener who begrudge me not at all my little bits of gallows jokery so long as I perform for them. Gotta perform. This has come to mean, it appears, that "I let people go." This morning I've had, well, today is a sort of a red-letter day when it comes to unemployment for many. Fraiser, Conclon, Truitt, DeWitt, and just now, Varney.

(He takes a long drink from his martini)

Who had come up through the International Division with me. I mean we started at the same time. Twenty some years ago. They *handed* him this entire market. All of North Africa. Handed it to him. And he blew it. His little thing? Little boys. Loved the little native boys. But it was not that which stalled his progress through the International Division. No.

(He sighs)

I did warn him. We had dinner last month in Nairobi. I said "Kroener and Mulcahey are going to want to see *something soon.*" A clear, clear *bloody* flat-out warning to this buffoon, and I did it as a favor to him because *we came up together.* But he kept going on and on about the little salesgirls he found, "nut-brown little milkmaid-gals," he called them. And implied a number of them were willing. And one sits there mortified, knowing, wanting to just get up and say, "Hey pal, nobody gives a fuck if your cock is twisted, just so long as the fourth-quarter profits are flyers."

(He wipes his brow. The heat of the room)

That is how we speak at World Headquarters. And you've gotta learn fast. What's funny to me is that they perceive me as some sort of gentleman farmer tending his little garden. "Oh call *Kenneth Hoyle,* he'll know how to handle *Varney.* He's marvelous at that sort of work." I'm good at firing people is what they're saying.

My first year of this particular assignment consisted almost exclusively of getting off of prop planes and doing "that sort of work." Because by the time Mulcahey and Kroener finally decided to let me have a shot at it, the orange bits on the lucite map had pretty much occluded our blue. And I was a sort of last-ditch-try-anything-what-about-Hoyle sort of thing.

The result has been a bit of a bloodbath. People who used to want to have a drink . . . they shy away a bit now. Do I blame them? You can't. Even though I don't make a game of it or take the slightest bit of pleasure out of the task. What sort of person would? But the thing to do is do it quickly. Because when you linger it's sheer hell.

In less than an hour the next batch starts trudging in. Less than an hour, next batch.

(Another martini is mixed)

This is how it's done. "Varney. It's no accident that I'm stopping off here in Tangier." And he looks at me. At first there is this moment of denial. The raw animal response—the instinct—"Do I run, do I hide?"

(He is quiet for a moment)

And I'll just sit very quietly. Because I want him to understand the thing that is happening and to create *an atmosphere of dignity.* Which is up to them. Before I have to utter the unfortunate words, "I'm here because we have to make a change." It's so much better when the words are not actually spoken.

But Varney, he gets it, he's an old hand. You know when it's over. So we sit here quietly. And then he asks me, "Doesn't it feel odd, Ken?"

"What?" I say.

And he says, "Your rise to power, Ken." And then he goes. Quietly goes. They go quietly when I do it.

And afterwards, when one is sitting by oneself here in one's room, it is not hard to think of the railroads to the ovens.

You do not want to talk about the ovens at World Headquarters. One time in the War Room, I made one of my little asides. I said I hoped that our baby-formula marketing policy in the Third World would not be looked upon as some sort of horrifying mercantile . . . Final Solution in twenty years. And Kroener looked at me over this huge table we have and said in his Havanaesque accent, "Well I hardly see the comparison between baby formula and Zyklon-B gas, do you?" Barks out a laugh. Which shuts me up. Quickly. Let me tell you.

(Pause)

When I told my wife that story, she said, "What I'd like to do is hang a big dead cow from one of the palm trees." At World Headquarters we have two giant palm trees in front of the building flanking the neon Iris and Rose sign that lights up Ocean Avenue in Santa Monica. So sometimes I think, "Well, why tell her these stories if she's going to be so hypersensitive?" But who else is there. To discuss this with. If not your mate? I mean, if not her, then . . .

(Pause)

Yeah, well. . . . Oh well. I will say this. I shocked her last winter in London. A young man who—well let me preface this—a lefty Brit with money. And when I say lefty you can safely read Stalinist. Which I really don't mind, I think it's cute, but not once has any of them apologized for having gotten it so very wrong for so many years and for having given the rest of the world such a bloody hard time all the while. Not once has any of them had the class to so much as stand up and say "Oh dear, oh sorry, we were wrong."

I have only one wish. That my father had been around to see Leningrad revert to St. Petersburg. I would have liked to have handed him that headline.

(He cuts and lights a cigar)

Anyhow. This Brit kid who works for us. We're at a party for the London office. Me. My wife, Barbara. Bunch of the guys. And the kid says to me, "Mr. Hoyle, sir," (and you know they're gonna fuck ya when they call you sir) "I must tell you I think that what we are doing in Africa is morally indefensible."

Well. I mean. There you are. His wife stands there grinning at me like a mad little Staffordshire terrier and there is my own wife, grinning, thrilling. And Kroener and Mulcahey taking it in too.

"Morally indefensible," I say. "How so?" And he sputters like a boiling tuber. "You've got saleswomen dressed up as nuns and *nurses* for God's sake running around *hospitals* in Lagos and Nairobi. You're treating baby formula in the Third World as if it's tonic water, which it is not, though by the time the mothers dilute it and the babies drink it, it may as well be. You've got billboards with *doctors* on them, for Christ's sake, proclaiming "Iris and Rose is better than breast milk." And the only reason you're getting away with any of this, Mr. Hoyle, is because you are doing it in a place where white people do not go on holiday. Come on," he says. "Defend *that*."

(Long pause. He smiles)

At World Headquarters you learn a kind of manufactured thuggishness. It is a sort of currency, if you will. The coin of our realm. It means nothing. Less than nothing. It's totally made up.

I look at the boy. "For years," I begin, "this company was run by uncomplicated men who had a clear goal: make a buck. And with the opening of so many world markets, it's taken these men a while to learn that you can't do business in Togo the same way you do in Elbow Lake, Minnesota." I stop for a moment. "'Cause in *Togo*, pal, things are different." What I'm doing is, I'm doing my gentleman farmer number. (Someone said poor Georgie Bush might have seen me on PBS, that documentary on corporate accountability, and stolen my style.)

Anyhow, back to the party. I say, "Listen. You and I both know that *you* know that. I can see from your tie that you did your hard time at the London School of Economics, so kiddo, clearly you're bright. Therefore, I'm not gonna stand here and play sandbox ethics with ya, so let me offer you this. Quit."

I take a breath. The room, it is glistening; it is limpid. He is beginning to look queasy but I'm not about to let this cocksucker off the hook. And this is where I got Mulcahey and Kroener. "If it's so very morally indefensible sitting here overlooking Green Park with your glass of stout and sausage on a toothpick, well then, this must be your resignation, and happy am I to accept it right here and now. Sir."

Exactly eighteen days later I was made Vice-President in charge of Marketing and Third World Affairs.

And like that. The reasoned apologia followed by the sucker punch. The boy, incidentally, never quit. Gave him Cairo and Libya, doing fine.

After the party, on the drive back to the hotel, Barbara said to me, "Did you have to do your Bugsy Siegel routine on that poor boy?" And I, without looking up from my *Financial Times*, said, "The little shit wants an ideological debriefing and some Altoid mints for his breath."

And silence until Claridges. Africa? Barbara says it has hardened me.

I seem to spend more and more time lately fending off a particular brand of self-satisfied righteousness. Mostly from women. Who think I will be shamed by a photo of a toddler with a swollen belly. And you know, you just find yourself retreating into a kind of manufactured Zen trance. It does no good to tell them I have *seen* swollen bellies. I have seen this face to face.

So what if Barbara has taken to imitating some of my bromides in a deeply Teutonic accent reminiscent of Henry Kissinger. I get the "choke." Because sometimes I have to apologize for the way in which we do business. But. When Barbara has toppled over the edge of bitterness into that realm in which careers are ruined, she will call me "the Albert Speer of baby formula."

I always know we're in tricky waters when I'm compared to some German or other. You see . . . I had some of our saleswomen in Africa dressed in sort of nurse's outfits. Pink. An error. A *mistake*.

And there's no winning with Barbara lately.

On the phone just now, when I tried to discuss this with her, she says, "You love bloodshed, don't you Kenneth." And I said to her, "Barbara. Have you ever had to work a day in your life. Have you? Because I do not think you know what it is to be simply afraid. Because I, Barbara, am *always* afraid."

And she says nothing. I go on. "My father, a card-carrying member of the party, sending me to communist summer camp in Peekskill, making me sing the Internationale with those lyrics about taking over the world.

"Barbara," I say. "I have been surrounded all my life by people who have to impose their earnest view of the world, this tidal wave of warm piss crashing down on me." I say, "At least, Barbara, in business there is a tangible measure of reality and achievement." And she says, "Chameleon. Lizard."

"Barbara," I say. "Please. We are not the Agency for International Development. We are no longer in the Peace Corps. We are not administering to the masses of the bloody *halt and the lame*. For God's sake, Barbara. It is business."

(*Beat*)

"Please." And she will not answer. She has nothing to say to this. This, after the great pleasure of waiting six hours for them to get you a phone line with an echo from Tangier to Santa Monica.

Marcus Hirshkovitz. My father.

Well of course I changed my name. "Vice-President Hirshkovitz"? What are you, nuts? I knew the world I was going into. And for many years Barbara would chide me gently about this. And I would ruefully laugh along with her because you've got to be thick-skinned in this world.

But I do try not to let politics get in the way of what is, at the core, a really good marriage. (Though for the both of us, the last election was a bit of a rough patch.) One night at dinner at Kroener's house for the managing director of the Australian subsidiary, we had on the Inauguration. And I turned to Barbara, she's still pissed off over this one, and said, "Barbara, dear, don't you feel betrayed by liberalism? They've managed to turn politics into a Hollywood award ceremony. Beverly Hills Earnest. Southern cracker glitz. Pesto and Big Macs." The Australians loved it. But they laugh at anything, those people, don't they?

Driving home, she turns to me and says, "Please. It's so vulgar using me to make points with the boys. You think they don't know? Don't ever do that again." Clenched teeth. I look over at her. "I apologize. I was being jocular. Playacting."

"Just keep your eyes on the road, Mr. Hirshkovitz," she says. That sharp, tight voice they use when they're mad. Wives.

I don't know. I think there is a point at which a particular kind of cruelty becomes meaningless. Becomes habit and it ceases to hurt. Because one is just so very tired of it.

Because one is just so very tired of it.

Let me ask you something: How do you go to work every day when everyone disapproves?

I had to go to *Geneva* last week. Yeah. Those godawful hearings at the World Health Organization. Screaming protesters outside the building. A Nestlé exec has a bucket of *blood* thrown on him. Turns out to be goat blood. A nightmare. A nightmare.

Well. Mulcahey and Kroener have given me the task of getting the boycott against us lifted. There are four countries which simply won't let our product off the docks. We can't even sell it. It's banned.

Did you see that piece about us on *60 Minutes*? My God. Us. Union Carbide and the Dalkon Shield. It was like Madame Tussaud's basement, for Christ's sake. All that was missing was the *Pinto.*

Anyway. I asked Barbara to come along because I saw it as

an opportunity to reaffirm something of the closeness we used to share readily. An inner life. . . . So. My speech to the World Health Organization. Or a bit of it. (This is after an exceptionally grueling slide show of some Ethiopian women who had misused the formula. A slide show in which the dead cattle and dead people seemed to have been shot with such insensitivity as to be interchangeable. I don't need to tell you about that.)

I said, "I think we were naive and we had a bottom-line sensibility and that is why we're here today. And perhaps we have been held unjustly accountable for the fact that the places we sell our product do not even have drinkable running *water* and governments which have no way of educating mothers living in dirt huts."

And I'm going on with this shuffle-and-dodge when . . . something happens. I see Barbara at the back of the room. Catch her eye. And I stop talking for a second. Everything is sort of . . . still, just for a moment. Well. Okay. Let's try something . . . different. And I drop my prepared remarks and I start again.

"I'm not sure," I tell the room, "if I have any more rationales left in me. When I dressed our saleswomen as nurses and put up billboards of doctors holding our formula, I knew what I was doing. All of us did. Because we're trained that any action is justifiable, if the results are profitable. And lately, I don't think I like that. I don't *like* being ashamed of myself. I don't *like* being ashamed of my industry. I don't *like* the way people look at me on airplanes when I tell 'em I'm in the baby formula business. *I don't like having to lie about who I am.*

(Beat)

Very strange, the silence. That Swiss silence. Very odd. And me—I feel something akin to a recklessness—similar to the

feeling one gets when one travels but without destination—
you could go anywhere.

By the time I'm done, I have, to my surprise, committed
us to changing the manner in which we market this product
all over the world. And there is silence. And then applause. I
have made a breakthrough—finally—something. I've done
something and there I am mobbed by my peers and I'm looking all over the hall for Barbara—where is she? Where has she
gone? She was standing there. *Why would she leave now?* And I
couldn't get out of that room—the crowd and it was so hot
in there and the photographers and all these people shaking
my hand and me smiling but where's Barbara, I don't want to
shake hands, please, please. I'm—I . . . just . . .

No more dead African babies. No more photos of bloated
stomachs thrust into my face every fifteen fucking minutes.
Please. Please. Please. Please. Please.

(Beat)

No more dead children. If you will.

(Beat. *He looks at something outside his window*)

What a sick, fucked-up country this is.

Afterwards, I met with Vilner. From the Nairobi office. A
German holdover from the old colonial days of this company when we were like some wandering pachyderm with
these ludicrous types in little offices boring everyone to death
all over the place. A dreadful man. The reports one gets.
Sauerbraten and beating the maid. But I had to drag him out
for the press as an implementor of my new policy.

In the bar, he sneers at me. "Hoyle. You will single-hand-
edly drag this company down. What you do not understand
is that there is no way to win in Africa. In Africa," he says,

"you must take whatever you can get, 'cause Africa, sooner or later, will kill you."

I nod. He's probably right. He's encouraged. "It's not that they are animals. Animals are, after all," he says, "cautious, prudent and economical. The African is none of these things."

Well. I mean. What can one possibly say to this? I say, "Maybe. But we've brought them the worst we've got to offer. The bottom of the barrel." I take a swig of whatever booze we are drinking. Barbara smiles at me. I smile back. And Vilner starts to look a little mean. "Und vott is the vorst, exactly Herr Hoyle?" And Barbara says drunkenly, "His name, actually, is Hirshkovitz." I smile again before answering Vilner. We are playing with razors. I say, "The worst? Booze, God, but mostly, Mr. Vilner, people like us. We are the worst the world has to offer. And you, sir, are right out of the bargain basement."

And there is silence for some time. "Hirshkovitz." He tries the name out like it's a little appetizer, a little bit of herring before the schnitzel. He's thinking he's got something on me he can use with Mulcahey and Kroener. "And does Head Office know how you feel?" (What he means is, "Do they know you're a hebe?") And I say, "Yes. And they are behind me. They support me utterly and without question. Everyone is behind me."

But they are not. And I sit for a moment. Get up. A little dizzy. Barbara looks at me. A little worried. God bless her. At least there is concern. And we walk outside. It is very late. Very very cold. And the lake is clear. Icy.

I want to say to Barbara, "I'm so tired, dear. I'm just so very tired. Please. Let's be civil. At least that?" I want to say, "I know everything you want to say but please do not say any of it."

But we walk silently. Stop at the newsstand. The International Herald Tribune has a picture of me making my pronouncements at World Health. And another of me talking to the protesters outside. It's very grainy. And a smile on me like a rictus. "Do I really look like that, Barb?" And she studies it for a moment and says to me, "Yes, Ken. I'm afraid you do."

Well. If I do. And if your conscience is a sword, a Damoclesian sword, well, let it drop. Let it fall.

And I think about Vilner. Head Office does not know how I feel. Barbara does not know how I feel. Why should they? How could they? "Does Head Office know how you *feel*?" (*Scornful*) Please. Vilner.

But he'll be by in a couple of minutes. And we're going to let him go.

Mulcahey and Kroener gave me the go-ahead.

Fire 'em all. And start from scratch.

(*Lights fade*)

PART TWO:

BE CAREFUL

ST. THOMAS, VIRGIN ISLANDS

*Afternoon. A cluster of pink stucco beachfront cabanas with green tin roofs—
all self-consciously quaint with hibiscus and palms giving privacy to each.
Inside a cabana sits Barbara Hoyle—in the near dark, under a ceiling fan.
She wears a faded indigo T-shirt, old jeans and sneakers.*

BARBARA: This morning I gave a speech to a group of wives.
"Wives of Executives Stationed in the Third World. Barbara
Hoyle, wife of Kenneth R. Hoyle (formerly of the Peace
Corps)."

Every two years my husband's company has this confer-
ence—a sort of baby formula summit. I couldn't go to the
last two. Which, Ken let it be known, was a hardship on him.

The first time we were invited was fourteen years ago and
of course, it was a signal that Ken was being "groomed."
"They're grooming you for the presidency," I would say, and
Ken would think I was teasing him, that I was making some
reference to his decision to leave the Peace Corps. Which,
sometimes, I think he still believes I hold against him.
Anyhow, five years ago, circumstances being what they were
at the time—

(There is a long silence here)

It seemed likely that Ken wouldn't go either, but at the last moment we concluded that it would be the best thing for us, for his career, our lives, if he went. After all. It had been a year since . . . Brazil. And Ken has always been able to look ahead. But that was the year that I was learning to cope with Brandon's being gone, after all, so I don't think the company held it against Ken that I didn't come. Maybe the second time I didn't show up, there were some whispers. Well. Ken told me there were some grumblings, so I knew I'd have to go this year and so I really did my homework and prepared and it's not so bad.

(*Beat*)

My speech went very well. Afterwards Doris Mulcahey and Ann Kroener came up to me to ask me to tea, and Doris— Doree—had tears in her eyes and said, "That was wonderful—I can't tell you how much you've contributed . . . " and Ann (who's always been so cold to me), she said—in that strong—steady—like a guy in a cigarette commercial—way, "Good to have you back Barb."

(*Pause*)

But to tell you the truth, I was very shaky, I was really in trouble.

My speech to young wives assigned to the Third World— the 3-W club, they call it—they have a little newsletter. I used to even write for it now and then when we were in Brazil. Mostly recipes—that's all they wanted really was mostly recipes and shopping hints.

(*Beat*)

My speech was entitled BE CAREFUL. Simply BE CAREFUL.

"I am happy to be speaking today to so many friends," I began. "Many of you are at this meeting on the eve of your first overseas assignment, indeed your first trip abroad, and are looking forward to it with some trepidation, if you are anything like me." A little laugh, a little titter. Actually, most of them are thinking "verandahs, pools, maids and expense accounts" is what occurs to me and then I push that out of my head—because you want to be fair to these girls.

(Beat)

They might have something going on, after all.

(Beat)

So I say to the girls—they like to be called that. Girls. I say to them, "Listen. There'll be outlets for you. Like the American Canadian Clubs with their Fourth of July picnics. Crochet classes, and pancake lessons for the maids."

I go on. "But I want to do something that we are encouraged to shy away from and I hope I do not make you uncomfortable. But you cannot discuss moving to the Third World without referring to the politics of what it means to be an American abroad." Anxious looks from Doris Mulcahey and Ann Kroener.

(Beat)

"We bring a lot of baggage with us." A safe beginning. "And sometimes we find ourselves in countries that we may disapprove of, but must do business in." I have learned never to say "our husbands must do business in. . . . " The wives like to be included in the commercial life of the company. "When we lived in Brazil, for instance, in the late 1970s and early

1980s, it was a military dictatorship. And the streets were overrun with the poor and the forgotten and many of them were younger than our own children . . . and let me tell you something—you've gotta learn to tell yourself 'This is not my business. This has nothing to do with me.' And because we are Americans—American women—to look at this injustice and harshness and simply—shut it out—that will be very difficult." I pause. "Because I know you are all sensitive people."

(Beat)

It was very quiet in the room now. I go on, now that I know I've got them—I'm giving them the straight dope. "You're gonna have to have dinner with some awful people, and you're gonna have to sit through some rough nights, and sometimes there will be men from the junta in your living rooms, as your children sleep in their bedrooms under ceiling fans, and these men drink a little of your scotch and you may say to yourself, 'Why should I be charming to this general?'

"And I say to you—this is why: because not to be does more harm than good—and I speak to you as equals—you women all have college degrees, and this has nothing to do with any partisan, you know, uh . . . "

(She shakes her head in disgust)

"All you can say to yourself is 'They do it differently in these places . . . '"

(Beat)

They nod. They know what they're in for. "And how do you explain these places to your kids?"

(Beat)

Silence. "Who have been brought up in a world of safety."

These women know of course, it's company mythology—about our son Brandon who was stabbed to death on Copacabana beach in broad daylight three days before we were to move back to L.A. Two months after he turned sixteen. Because Ken and I had given him a shiny watch for his birthday. And he stupidly wore it to the beach. A diver's watch. Hence the title of my speech to the "Wives of Third World Execs." Be careful.

(Beat)

I don't say anything about this. That would not be appropriate and I have come here determined to help my husband—you see—it is rumored, he tells me, that he is to be named "President of the International Division" when Mulcahey retires next month—at the age of seventy-eight. This is why I am here. To see if I can hold up.

(Beat)

Under the *stress* of such a situation. And Ken has told me there are spies in the room. "When you give your speech—remember—it's a test." But he doesn't ask to hear it—that would be . . . he's not that kind of man. Not a nervous, undignified climber.

And I have always loved that about him. I do believe that for all of his . . . faults, he is not a man who would do something undignified in order to get ahead.

Right now, he is at a planning session. "The Corporate Conscience in the New Third World." That's the title of his lecture. He said to me this morning, "These guys'll sit there, they'll feel good, but it's me who has to sit in the Minister of Health's waiting room, swatting flies and making jokes." And I said, "Ken, wait a second, are you unhappy?" And he rolls his eyes. We don't have much money saved. So leaving is a . . .

(She shakes her head)

I understand this. You know, I said to the girls, "Be careful that the company perks don't give you unrealistic expectations of wealth, because, you know, the house and the car and the servants are not yours and when you come back home you will not be able to afford them, unless . . . "

(Beat)

"You come from money." This is good advice. I had a wonderful job. Before we left.

(There is a silence)

Taking pictures. At the studios, I was in the stills department but you can't get back in, you just can't, once you've gone. Those jobs are not. . . . They don't just sit about going, "Oh, when is Barbara Hoyle coming back from Africa or Brazil?" They hire their cousin. Ken will sometimes go, "Well then, why don't you go back to Paramount taking pictures of Steve McQueen?"

(Beat)

"Steve McQueen isn't making movies anymore," I say. "You know that." And he goes, "Exactly." Ah . . . it was a silly job, I know, and it was a frivolous world, that was, that commissary . . . but . . . it actually, it was a sort of harmless one given the . . .

(*Pause*)

There was a lot, of course, that I left out because it is certainly not my intention to sabotage my husband's career. I could have gone on all day to the girls on the subject of "be careful." I might have said, "Do not have an affair with a subordinate of your husband's." But knowing Ken, he would have fired Travis anyway. For Ken I think firing people has become a sort of prayer but. . . . Okay. Travis. Okay, well, there were these *dinners*. By their pool. Hmn. The night he said to me— while Ken and Julia were at the house and we were walking on the beach, "Your husband does not love you, does he Barbara?" And I said, "What are you talking about?" And then, before he said anything, I put my hand to his mouth and said, "Don't. If we are going to have anything, please let it not be at my Kenneth's expense, not as a reaction against him. Too much that I have is simply a response to Kenneth."

We would meet at the Oyster Box Hotel—way up the coast, way out of town. Beach and sugarcane fields and bungalows. Some people have affairs in order to pretend, in order to forget. For Travis and me it was a spur to memory, it was— in the cabana, sandy and gritty and wet after lovemaking— that was who we really were, and I would lie there on top of the bed with him, listening to the surf and think of my son— because—he . . .

(*Beat*)

Was the product of a real passion. Travis, losing his hair, paunchy, winded—nothing like Ken. "Brandon would like Durban." That statement, made to Ken at dinner, the evening after my eighth liaison with Travis, gave me away. Because we never ever spoke of Brandon. Because to speak of Brandon was to talk of love. And Ken put down his fork, and he looked at me, and he knew.

"Why would you say that?" Ken asks. "What do you mean?" And I say nothing. Go on to my osso bucco—we have a cook working for us who served an Italian exec before we caught him. "Prize," said one of Ken's lieutenants over calamari one night. "A treasure."

(Beat)

I say this to them and I mean it, I want to help. "Be careful of spending too much time alone. Learn the language— whatever you do—learn the language fast. The silence in those houses they find for you with the servants—it can overwhelm you." I smile. A sister. "Look. I'm gonna level with you,"—now I know I'm really hitting my stride, doing a sort of a midwife routine—"they say it's an adventure and it is. But it's also a sacrifice. You're giving up things here and when you come back, it'll never be the same—make sure your husband understands this. Make sure he knows that what you're coming back to is not the . . . "

(Pause)

"Of course, not all of you will come back with a dead son."

(Beat. She smiles sadly)

Have I crossed a line? I never talk about this. But it seems false—mealymouthed not to make mention of it—and I—to tell you the truth—I am beginning to realize it is expected of me.

I go on. "Most likely, percentage-wise very few of you will

come back without a child—but if you do . . . come back . . . with a coffin . . .

(Beat)

"Talk about it." They nod. They know. They're women for God's sake, not just DARs. I shake my head. "You know—we hear the news. 'We're moving overseas.' Maybe we're sitting in the kitchen alone after they've gone to the office, having that quiet cup of afternoon coffee and the phone rings and it's your husband and he says, 'I was right. We're going to . . . Surinam or Sri Lanka or Rio.' And there is this sense of . . . 'oh, it's a mission . . .' that sort of overtakes you. A dream.

"Remember, it is not . . . your mission. Your husband's mission is not—your mission. Be careful . . . that you keep the clarity of your own life." I pause. They are nodding. "Or you will come back and you will have . . . dust. You will have nothing." Silence.

(Pause)

"In Rio, there are open-air meat markets and they wrap the sides of beef with newspaper—so it's all flies and blood and the air is sticky and thick. So when I say 'be careful' it is— that—when we had to make arrangements for Brandon, what I remember is the street.

"Not my son.

" . . . So be careful that—your memory is clear and intact because when I think of Brandon—the first thing I see are the sides of beef on the sidewalks of Copacabana."

(Beat)

"So the memories you have should be guarded, because I think that is a very great loss. The greatest loss. . . ." I seem to, I . . . don't remember the girls in the room now—just a sense—of calm. I was standing and I sat down. There was a chair on the podium and I sat and had a glass of water before speaking again.

"Maybe there is another loss to guard against, if possible, I don't know myself how you do it." And I told them about Kenneth.

(Pause)

"The man I married and the man who sold baby formula to African mothers without regard to the consequences," I suggested, "are not one and the same. I do think—since I have been asked to speak to wives assigned to the Third World, that the baby formula business should be addressed. It would be squeamishly Pollyannaish of me if I simply bypassed this issue that has been such a part of our lives in this company.

"The death of our son," I tell them, "somehow gave my husband . . . an opening. I am sure we all—I take it for granted that you agree that not only was our company a perpetrator of an evil, but worse—fought back when confronted and vigorously contested all efforts to halt that wrong, and that none of us would support such a policy today and that those mistakes were made by the husbands of another generation who are now being put out to pasture and replaced by more enlightened practitioners of trade and export. . . ." And I go on. "But my husband actually designed the marketing policy for the Third World, and. . . ." Here I believe I pointed to Ann Kroener and Mrs. Mulcahey. . . ."And the reason your husbands gave the job to Kenneth was because they understood that he had, after Brandon died in Rio, turned to stone and could do anything. And so, ladies," I concluded, "most importantly, be careful that the company does not turn your husband into something unrecognizable until it is too late . . ."

(She begins to pack)

This is a nice island. They've picked a few losers in the past—one year it was the Grand Cayman and there were lots of banking jokes making the rounds and the beach was riddled with sand fleas so . . . that was the first year I went.

(Beat)

Brandon was seven years old . . . and he scrambled in the sand, and Ken and I had been out of the Peace Corps a few years—he said to me—we were in a hammock between two palms, "This is where the world will get changed. Us. People like us will be the ones." And he held my hand. Brandon in the sand, running around.

Be careful of stupidity. One's own. Girls. Because sitting there that day in the sand, all of us together, I chose to believe him, which in retrospect was perhaps a bit of a mistake.

(She smiles, thinks)

And I explained this to the women this morning, and my feeling is they were grateful. They were grateful that some-one could say these things, and that there is so much that's endurable, and I was pleased to give them that. And there was a real connection. I could tell that they had all listened—even if they had, except for Kroener and Mulcahey, been too shy to say anything to me. But—at their age, I would have been too.

I would have liked to have . . .

(She stops for a moment)

Just sat with some of them afterwards. Maybe gone into the dining room and just let the afternoon wind away and I guess

I'm a little disappointed that none of them . . . but probably they were going on the tour of the old sugar mill on the other side of the island.

That is the afternoon event.

(*Barbara stands for a moment before putting on her sunglasses, picking up her suitcase and exiting into the glaring afternoon sun. Lights fade*)

PART THREE:

THE DAY OF THE DEAD

A corner room at the Hotel Principal, Oaxaca, Mexico. Hoyle sits on the bed. Hair shorter, old well-worn pants. A tape recorder beside him is on. A number of maps, pocket atlases atop the bed. Evening.

HOYLE: You have to drink bottled water here. And it's a nice discipline. You have to conserve unless you want to keep asking the man at the desk downstairs to bring more, and he's far too old. Though the fact is, people here in Mexico are far too gracious to complain. One of the many lovely qualities here.

(Beat)

The first time we came down here, our honeymoon—to this hotel. Barbara stood in the courtyard and said to me, "If ever I should disappear. . . ." And I said "What? You'd come here?" And she said, "Yes. This is where I'd come."

What a thing to say on a honeymoon. So portentous, eh? And what about me? Silly. To sit here waiting for her. As if . . .

I mean, we know how big the world is, so. . . . But, I mean, she's gotta be somewhere, right? And it's true, Mexico has always been a place we've escaped to. Escaped to. One of those places where you can actually locate yourself. A singular rugged integrity, an openness. And really, I have never met, in all my travels, a more courtly, decent people than the Mexicans. They go out of their way to act kindly.

Anyway. I thought she might like to know, she should know that I resigned from the company and . . .

(*He smiles, shakes his head*)

Why do I do that? Now? To lie? What is that? You see, that's not strictly true. What happened, of course, is . . . they fired me. (How could they not, given that fiasco of a day on St. Thomas.) After Barbara deep-sixed my career in one magnificent end run. I am finding, to my surprise, that not working is . . .

(*Beat*)

Not without its . . . pleasures.

Dear Mother. If only you knew, over there at the Jewish Home for the Aged in Baltimore—but an hour ago, I was in the town square, the zocalo, which was filled with old peasant women, and whenever I see peasant women, lately, I find myself thinking of you. Because, let's face it, you were no debutante, in your kitchen, boiling a chicken.

For some reason, because, perhaps, so much of Mexican life is about family, you're on my mind. And the company was probably a bit of a mom for me.

When I come back to the States I should really come and see. . . . I . . . the brochure makes it seem a lovely place.

(*Beat*)

I wish there was a way I could specify when, but my plans are so . . .

(*Beat*)

Unformed right now.

Thank Christ you no longer understand any of this, thank God you've gone back to Yiddish. It must be very pleasant to leave English behind in your dotage. Maybe Cousin Ruth, or Bea, or *one* of those cousins that I never really could get straight, maybe one of 'em will translate this nicely for you. I mean. If you even recognize the voice.

Do you know how they fired me? I mean, let me tell you, they waited a reasonable amount of time after Barbara's speech. They waited about three hours.

She was on the ferry to St. John when I caught up with her. Mother. It was the kind of day that you know actually exists somewhere in your life but when it descends on you to flatten you, you go "Oh. I see. So this is it. It's here. This is the worst. The very worst." And I've had two. Two such days. Two. Not so painful as I feared.

I've always wondered Mother, what the day was like when you left Odessa. You certainly never talked about it. Listen to me. Casting about for a history. Now. At this late date. Silly.

Anyway, I get back to the hotel, Barbara having insisted that I let her have the day. "Just please, Ken, a day for myself. I cannot think." She said.

She found a beach on St. John called "Salt Pond." A lunar and deserted place, it figures she would love it. Well what was I supposed to do? Pull her off the ferry by her hair? Maybe I should have. Anyway Mulcahey and Kroener called me into their suite. They had taken a suite as their command center. The Pompano Room or the Triggerfish Suite. Something.

Whatever it is, that unmistakable smell of an expensive hotel. No matter where in the world. That has become repulsive to me. Simply unendurable since then.

And Mulcahey starts. "There was a scene with your wife."

"Yes," I say. "I know."

Kroener, oddly, looks bored. Looking out into some middle space out over the Caribbean waiting to come in for the kill.

"I'm sorry about Barbara." I began. "The event triggered a very specific response in her." They don't move, these two men. Not a sign. Nothing. "There were memories," I say. "She was reminded of Rio. It was a mistake to ask her to do this, I'm so sorry." And, you know, I'm thinking, "I should not do this. I should not try for their pity, they ain't got any, you know that Ken, come on."

Mom. You don't know about Kroener. He's from Havana, and his family owned practically every tobacco plantation there or something, and they lost it all, so he's forever flying off to Boca Chica to plot the next assassination attempt against poor old Fidel. So being at a Caribbean resort had him all hopped-up.

And the man *never* liked me. (A Jew hater? No. Just never liked me.) He had that true sociopath's instinct for other people's weaknesses. And Barbara, of course, was mine.

I should have known that when they wanted to get to me, they'd do it through Barbara.

(Beat)

(Quiet) "Maybe I did know?" you wanna ask. Well. Maybe. Maybe.

Mulcahey really *had* to retire *sometime* soon, he had this ongoing war with prostate cancer and gin and, you know . . . I was clearly next in line.

And of course, Kroener wanted it all for himself, the whole candy store.

(Beat)

From Dad, I got one thing, I'm a pretty good fighter. And I used to joke to myself that motion was everything to a guy like me. So standing there in the Pompano Suite, what was running through my mind was "Forget Kroener, you can't beat him. Can Mulcahey be turned?" An Irish brute and deadly but he'd been mildly drunk on rum since volleyball at dawn on the beach.

"Donald," I said looking at him. "Where's the harm? So she said things. So what? Where's the lie? Well? Well aren't we a little bit dirty? What company isn't?" I said this. I said, "You're not such a company man yourself, we've sat in the bar at Musso's, bitching and moaning, right?" He smiles. I go on, you know, encouraged. "Maybe it was healthy, what she did? and besides, pal, are the wives such delicate flowers that they can't stand to hear the truth about us?"

(Beat)

"And it is the truth about us." That's what I said. Yeah. I mean, I was quite upset. And I said, "This company can and must change. And you know it. And I know it. And all Barbara did was speak it aloud and plainly and that . . . ain't . . . so bad."

Mulcahey—he gets it. And he looks at Kroener, you know, a raised eyebrow, palm out, as if to say, "Hell, the guy's right, Octavio."

(Pause)

I go on. "My wife has suffered. My wife has endured. My wife has . . . "

And Kroener says, a shrug, a smile, "All our wives have suffered. It means nothing. That, Ken, is what they do." And a long silence.

And I'm thinking "I will not trash my wife for these men, I will not do it. Not now. No, no, no. No."

And Kroener turns away, looking off in the general direction of Havana and says, "It cannot be borne. And it shall not be." And in his hand, this miserable corporate Iago is holding a manila file. "Your retirement package. Read it. Sign it, and we'll be done." Hands me his Mont Blanc.

(Beat)

Listen, you know, Mom, you don't know the business world, but, let me tell ya, it's not like they were generous. It was a very reduced pension.

And God, I will admit, I did regret, for the first time in my life, not having taken advantage of the ceaseless offers of bribes and kickbacks because now, after twenty-some-odd years, I'd have amassed a cold couple of mil or so in Lucerne, let me tell ya, and you would not be in a double at the Jewish Home for the Aged . . . in Baltimore . . .

And I stand there. My legs shaking. "I see." I turn to Mulcahey. And he looks miserable, sodden. Pissed. "Ken," he says, "don't fight it, it's a fair package considering you're out early, you're a young guy." He says this to me, "You got plenty of time to get on your feet . . . "

I stand there. Say nothing. I stand there smiling, smiling. You know, like, if I'm reasonable, well, it'll all be okay. Schmuck.

(Beat)

I used to wonder what they were thinking when I did it.

(Beat)

You know. Kroener and me, I think about it now, we share a kind of madness. I don't know if you'll understand this at the Jewish Home for the Aged in Baltimore, but, the madness we share is that he, like me, does not think that other people are actually real.

Really exist. So it makes it possible to do any number of awful things. Any number of . . . orders . . . to follow. Because nobody is really real. Isn't that nuts? And then, you know, Kroener and Mulcahey did something really terrible. They brought in their wives. To bear witness. Doris Mulcahey and Ann Kroener.

Who had actually taped Barbara's speech. And I knew then, that I just couldn't fight it. It's a meticulous kind of viciousness and it was, as you may expect, quite successful.

(He plays the tape)

BARBARA'S VOICE: The death of our son must have finally given to my husband a kind of permission to become this Albert Speer type. He likes to joke that I had the wrong German: He was more of a Kissinger. The Kissinger of baby formula. Kroener, the Nixon. Anyhow, the point is, the man I married and the man who marketed this despicable product to African mothers are not one and the same. So be careful that this company does not do the same to your husband. It's too much to lose . . .

(Hoyle switches off the machine and stares out for a moment before exchanging tapes)

HOYLE: Not much left to say after that, is there?

(Beat)

So I just stood there. Actually, I started to cry. A little bit. A little. Now, I mean, if Kroener is in fact like me, you know none of it meant a thing. And I'm crying, thinking, "Why does this matter so much, why, why, why does it matter at all . . . ?" Crying.

But. Doris Mulcahey looks at me. And she takes my hand, and she says something to me that I will never forget for the rest of my life. She says, "Ken. You know something. You've got to be nuts to stand here in this room talkin' to these men."

She says this to me. And please. Let me tell you. It is the most extraordinary moment of my professional life. Because someone was being human. Which was the *last* thing I expected there.

She says, "Don't do this. Leave. It's better for you. And it's better for Barbara. *That's* where you need to be now. Not here." And the room is silent. She looks over at her husband, who is this writhing, cancerous snake, and she looks at him with a kind of infinite pity. She's still holding my hand. This marvelous woman that I never knew. (*Angry*) There are people like that. I know it. There are.

(*Beat*)

And she walks over to Kroener. And she strokes his hair. He does nothing. And she says to me, "One day, someone will do this to him. And there will be, I promise you, no one to protest it." She smiled. "At least you have that."

And with that, I signed the papers and I walked out of the room, and onto the beach. The sun beating down. White. Sand was white. And I waited for Barb.

And I'll tell you this. The vulgar subterfuge of my dismissal will linger always. I will say this: I came of age in hotels. I drew comfort from them and when I fired people, or made some sort of bad deal, I did it in a hotel; for some reason, in a hotel, nothing sticks. It's all transitional and you're never stuck with the vital you. The vital self of a guy in his home, right? Mom? Whatever *that* is?

And if I had fired myself, I would not have gone out of the way to lure me to the Pompano Suite on St. Thomas. I would not have gone out of my way to humiliate.

After all. When my son died, did I not continue? Kroener? You swine.

A watch. For a watch. And Barbara and I flying back with the body. Why did I go back to work?

I always hated our product.

Well Mother. The world is so large and so un . . . tameable, really. Who will ever know what one is responsible for in this world. When—when—when I caught up to Barbara at the ferry I was at least, before she pushed me away—able to say "I'm sorry, I'm sorry, I'm . . . sorry . . ."

(Pause)

It is the Day of the Dead here in Oaxaca. And in Mexico, you know, Mom, they don't fear the dead, they don't look at death as a loss. It's an occasion for rejoicing. And I think that is what drew us here so often.

Here in Oaxaca, they sell "death-bread" in the bakeries— little brioches topped with icing in the shape of shinbones. There are kids urging their parents to buy them little sugar skulls and there are little skeletons, they give these as gifts. They prepare dishes for their own dead, who are supposed to swoop down and eat them at night.

And if the dead are children, Mother, "angelitos," little angels, if they happen to be children, honey, cakes, milk and fruit are placed on the altar.

I find that extremely . . .

(Pause)

And I must say, I am sure, sure, I am quite certain that Barbara will come.

It's funny, dear Mother, here in Oaxaca, in the zocalo, as the old women were getting ready for the Day of the Dead, I was thinking, "How nice it might be to be protected again." And I wanted to write. Oh, ludicrous. You're eighty-nine years old and you don't even have your teeth. You don't know anything anymore and according to cousin Ruth, are a child yourself, but still . . . wouldn't it be nice to take me in? Mother?

(Beat)

(Very quiet) Back home. That would be nice. Barbara. You. Brandon. Brandon.

(He goes to the window, looks out at the Day of the Dead procession approaching and begins to sing, very softly, a Yiddish lullaby)

Four Monologues

First produced at Naked Angels in New York City in November 1991 as part of a program designed to spotlight the political pressures brought to bear on the National Endowment for the Arts. Joe Mantello directed the following cast:

Standards & Practices . . . . Rob Morrow
Library Lady. . . . . Rose Gregorio
The Girl on the Train. . . . . Lili Taylor
Broadway. . . . . Geoff Nauffts

STANDARDS & PRACTICES

A sharp-looking young man is seated in a director's chair, fiddling with his Armani suit.

They say a lot about the "integrity vacancy" in my profession, which is television. Networks . . . that's my particular area. Standards and practices.

(Shrugs)

You find yourself listening to these people. Decent people, but they don't have to face the unwashed masses the way I do in standards and practices. I mean, we're lawyers, you know? I'm no artist.

(Beat)

I have no pretensions about it, I have to deal with Colgate-Palmolive and Proctor & Gamble and Nestlé and General Foods, and these are decent types, these are decent guys. Lawyers, okay, so you get the picture.

(Beat)

A little dry, maybe, a tendency to look at things as simply as black and white, but after years of having to go through law school, it's not hard to lose your sense of humor.

(Beat)

But ask yourself this: Who is out there calling the shots? You know? I mean, I really, really despise petty moralizing, I really do.

(Beat)

And a lot of what I'm asked to do is fatuous even to me, and there is no doubt you could laugh at me—a Jew—smart, you know, you can look at a guy like me and say, "He inherited his liberalism," because I have not lived through anything.

But I'll tell you something, and please, anyone who disagrees with this is—gotta be living in another world. . . .

When you reach the age of about twenty-seven to thirty-two, you basically, you've had to make all the moral choices. . . .

There is nothing you don't have to confront. So listen—I want to ask you this— Who out there is calling the shots? Because let me tell ya, if ya think it's us guys at standard and practices, I can promise you this: You—are—wrong.

If you think it's the guys at Proctor & Gamble, you—are—wrong.

(Beat)

Because, basically, what we are, we are men and women who sell certain things. But let me tell you: We get letters, and I mean, they are filled with rage. They are filled with a . . . a

. . . a passionate anger toward . . . this coast. This business. What we do. They hate us. So much. Letters from people offended by homosexual acts. AIDS on the Movie of the Week. There are people who are fueled by this.

(Beat)

And I read these letters and I want to take a shower.

(Beat)

People who have this agenda. But they get together, they send these letters to the decent lawyers at Proctor & Gamble, who get scared, and they call me.

(Beat)

We get letters. There is a tide of hatred out there, and you cannot understand it, you cannot fathom the depths. This is a country filled with letter-writers; people who stay up all night, writhing and twisting, people who drive very old cars and have the strangest of habits, and people who have no real control over those habits. This country has a seam of absolute maniacal viciousness, and let me tell you—because you are all really—we're in the same boat—it's you and me against the treyf out there—understand this:

They are stronger than us; they outnumber us, and they are angrier than we are; and they do not care about your—your "environment," your "freedom of speech," they want to kill. They want to kill your faggot brother, they want your sister to have that baby, and they—and they—are the people who buy all the shit I sell every night.

(Beat)

I have to make the world smooth for them.

(Beat)

That is my job.

(Beat. *Very quiet*)

When you hit—you know, age about twenty-eight, you have to make just about every moral decision there is to make.

(Beat)

Like today. Two men kissing?

(Beat)

I had them cut it.

(Beat)

Anything that disturbs the beast out there. No way.

(Beat)

Just think of me as one of the guardians of your safety; I keep the animals happy. Because they will take over the zoo if we let 'em.

(*Picks up the phone*)

Get me Colgate.

LIBRARY LADY

A middle-aged woman at a desk, surrounded by too many books.

The other day, they had a lecture. Upstairs, in the Oak Room, which was donated by Mrs. Hamilton Straight when we did the renovations and additions fourteen years ago.

I went. I stood there, in the back. An author speaking. An author; they thought, "Let's have culture—after all, this is a library for God's sake, a library ought to have a little culture."

And when they asked me, they said, "Hildy, we were thinking, a lecture series for the Oak Room might be nice, what do you think, dear?" This was Arlene Sagitt, from the Board of Education. I said, "Depends on the books, honey, you know?"

(She goes back to her book for a moment, stamps a little rubber library stamp on the front page)

Three weeks late. It's my biggest problem. I'm the one that gets blamed, I'm the one that gets . . . well, frankly, I'll say this: There are one or two books that I wouldn't mind if they'd never bring them back. Just keep 'em out forever.

Wouldn't even send them an overdue notice, just quietly look the other way.

Certain books.

They can have 'em. Though I do wonder what they do with them for so long. Do they just keep them on their bedside tables? And pick them up late at night?

And what do they do with these books? I ask myself. What?

(*Beat*)

Nobody wants to ask the hard questions, nobody wants to ask these questions, not like when I first came to this library; there were different . . . book . . . standards.

(*Pause*)

More in keeping with . . . well, you know what happened yesterday? At the lecture? He read poetry.

Some people, they don't care what they say, they say, "Oh, well, I have thoughts, I have . . . ideas." I say, keep your ideas to yourself, why don't you?

Because that is what people with manners are trained to do, like Nick Carraway at the beginning of The Great Gatsby says, "Some people are born with no manners and you just have to forgive them; they haven't had the same advantages as you."

The poet? He said a whole lot. He said a lot. I can tell you.

(*She looks down at a piece of paper, looks up, triumphant*)

And I'm not like the biddies, the old wives that volunteer. I'm a with-it gal, I think, but I don't know, I have an idea of appropriate and not and—I don't mind repeating the words, the bad words, the four-letter words even, you know, when they start talking about the Lord.

(She smiles, shakes her head)

So, they think, Oh, someone like— What am I? The house-wife in Kansas City? They think someone like me, that I am stupid and pious and have lumpy ankles and a Ph.D. in Dewey Decimal.

(She picks up a book, looks around the room, and stuffs it in her purse)

So, lately, what I've been doing, I'll tell you, is, I just don't know, maybe it's wrong, but I get rid of them, if they offend me. Because we've been—they make us feel dumb, if we say anything, we get these snickers, intellectual guffaws: "Oh, your values mean nothing."

(Pause)

We did have a nice lecture a month ago; a man came from the college to talk about *Paradise Lost*.

(Beat. She smirks)

My idea, and of course, you know, you get a very thinking crowd, a very . . . some serious people, and it might not have been the biggest turnout, but people wanted to hear about the fall of man from grace, they wanted to think about their actions.

(She smiles at the audience)

I have a list.

(Beat)

This library, it'll be a warm well-lit place, for decent people, who have open minds and charitable hearts. People like you and me.

(*She puts another book in her bag after looking around*)

But first I have to get rid of the filth. Don't you agree?

THE GIRL ON THE TRAIN

A young woman in a bulky sweater, her legs tucked under her, sits staring out the window of a train on the New Haven line.

Just a few days ago, for instance, I was on the train from Meriden, just the other day, the Amtrak, you know, and there was a man.

Much older man, and really thinned out, and I knew he was in trouble, because he was all alone and he had one of those manila envelopes. The kind they put X-rays in, and it said "Property of . . . " some hospital in some little town in Vermont. He kept biting his knuckle, and he was sitting right across from me.

And there was also a lady, much older also, and I carried her bag to the rear car that goes to Alexandria, Virginia, and she needed help.

It was too hard to do alone.

A train is a place where you find men and women who like to be helped.

(She smiles, shakes her head, looks down at the floor)

You don't know what they're like, or who they are, what they do, but they're vulnerable on a train.

And I guess what happens is, it makes you think better of them. That there are decent people in this country. I mean, I say that at home, in New York, and you know it's foolish. I say it at dinner with my boyfriend. He paints. . . . I say, "I think there are decent people here." He smirks. I say, "No really, you know, we're drowning in pesto in this city, we're, I feel like we're just drowning in our smugness and . . . " And he looks at me. "Are you saying that my art is *rarified?*" he says.

And I say, "No, no, but we sit around and we make fun of other people's values." He says nothing to this. "There are other values," I say, "certain things mean something to other people and, okay, fine, we want to be left alone to live our lives, but I certainly can understand why a cross marinated in urine might cause anguish, and to make fun of the people who are anguished is to me—narrow-minded and . . . small."

He says nothing to this.

Actually, he says to me, "Martha, you know what your problem is, your problem is you have a daddy fixation. Like all Catholic girls from Mineola, you want to do the right thing."

I say nothing.

"Martha," he says, "you're disfiguringly . . . conventional."

(*Pause*)

I've been taking the train a lot lately because Manhattan has gotten so close, you know what I mean? And that decency— that you look for—well, it's always a surprise when you find it in the city.

I do sometimes meet my dad for lunch, and sometimes he says things to me, and I know what he means. He gave me that book by that woman who wrote speeches for the president, and I kept saying to myself, "Yes, she's right." When she said she was offended by the people on the bus with her to Washington in the sixties, because they made fun of the soldiers who were fighting for her, I knew what she meant.

My dad gave me that book.

You know, and he said, he said "Martha, I think you'll like this, you're a lot like her." Which I'm not.

Sometimes I have dinner with a group of my boyfriend's friends, and we sit at Florent and I just want to—I just want to scream because I feel so—out of touch. "There are other values," I say to them, "besides . . . I don't know, aesthetics."

I am confused. I know that. I know I am. Please. I— He dragged me to that thing for the guy running against the senator, I mean we all know who I mean, and it was—it was just awful. It was filled with the worst people, and I didn't identify with—

(Beat. She shakes her head. A whisper)

I just didn't. And I thought, You know, this guy's home state is filled, it's got to be the poorest, the—the most helpless— what do they care about art? Why should they?

(Pause)

Maybe I like the train because when you're in motion in this country, when you're traveling, you don't have to decide. You can help people with their bags, you can help people get a cup of coffee when they're scared and alone and their X-rays—You can watch the fall colors whirr by outside your window in a blur and you don't have to make those decisions.

(Beat)

About what you believe in.

BROADWAY

Dressed in black leather jacket, black jeans, and heavy black boots, a young man stands with his back against a chain-link fence. He carries a boom box and is smoking a cigarette.

Before Kevin died he said to me, "What're you going to do with all those awful old records of mine?" I said, "Well, what do you want me to do, exactly, with *Chorus Line* and *Brigadoon* and, uh, *Carousel*, Kev?"

And he said, "Shit, maybe you should learn 'em all by heart, 'cause you're probably gonna have to do the revivals if you wanna eat."

And we laughed. He was dying; it's really funny how easy it is to laugh when you're dying. He said, "Alex, it's fine that we lost our grant, who needs a militant homo company of dancers in this country?"

I don't have an answer for that. I used to think I did, actually. I mean, I really did. We lost our grant last week, the NEA dropped us, but I don't think it was 'cause we were a homo company, what do you think?

(Beat)

One by one this company is getting smaller. Paul is a waiter, and he splattered oil from some soft-shell crabs or something and is . . . looking for another—uh, let's see, you know, six—there are six of us—dead.

(*Pause*)

It's hard to dance on AZT.

(*Beat. Quiet*)

We had a space a lot like this one, we were friends, just a bunch of us, and why did we dance? I mean, we lost our space. I haven't seen— How many of us are left? After Kevin? Eight.

(*Beat*)

We don't even like to see each other, there's nothing left to say, I mean, Jerry was trying to get a job on *Meet Me in St. Louis* and—

(*Pause. Quiet*)

Last year—he would not have had to dance for those people, or sing or smile; last year we did not have to pretend to be happy chorus boys. You know? But you start misjudging the world.

(*Beat*)

This morning I actually, I sat down and listened to all those musicals of Kevin's, and I'll tell you they were very pleasant, they were just great.

(*Beat*)

Fuck it, I threw 'em all out. Maybe the NEA is right. Maybe
we were promoting homoeroticism. Yes, *sure* we were. I
thought, Hey, it *needs* a little promoting, they're still bashin'
people's heads in, you know, and—it needs a little promoting; we got guys dragging each other out of the closet and
into the tabloids.

(*Beat*)

It needs a little promoting, you know. But I misjudged, I really did.

(*Beat*)

I said to Kevin, over at Sloan-Kettering, right before he went,
I said, "Shit, man, if I'd only known. We should've been promoting *Jerome Robbins' Broadway*. That's where the money is."
Kevin laughed. But that's always been my problem: I'm
behind the times. Fuck it.

COQ AU VIN

First produced at Naked Angels in New York City in December 1991 as part of a program to benefit Amnesty International, the human rights organization. Joe Mantello directed the following cast:

Chicken One .... Patrick Breen
Chicken Two .... Bradley White
Man .... Garreth Williams

Lights come up on two people in chicken suits, center stage.

CHICKEN ONE: Cunts. Cheap, miserable, brassy, lowdown, good-for-nothing, sadistic, cheating cunts.
CHICKEN TWO: Please don't cause a scene. I beg of you.

(Chicken Two does a little chicken dance)

CHICKEN ONE *(Sotto voce, scornful)*: We're supposed to be *happy.* Happy. Hah! Look at you.

(Chicken Two does nothing—except try to look dignified)

You're beneath contempt. Not even to protest. Not to raise your voice like I have. To sit silently and let it happen to you, it's disgusting.
CHICKEN TWO: Look who's talking, pal.
CHICKEN ONE: And what exactly is that supposed to mean?
CHICKEN TWO: Quiet! They'll catch us! Then where'll we be? Then what?

(They make little pecking motions and chicken noises)

I'm just happy to participate.

CHICKEN ONE (*Mimics in a pansy voice*): I'm just happy to *par-tic-ipate!* God, you make me sick to my stomach. To think that you talked me into this.

CHICKEN TWO: Yeah, you and your busy schedule. You! You haven't worked in a year and a half.

CHICKEN ONE: That's right, I haven't. That's precisely correct. Exactly. And why have I not worked? In a year and a half?

(*Beat*)

CHICKEN TWO: I don't care to discuss it.

CHICKEN ONE: That is what they've done to us. Reduced us to chickens at the County Fair. Yes. You know, I mean, I have to actually laugh because no training, you know, not the Royal Academy or Strasberg or that bitch Adler could have ever, *ever* prepared me for this: Reduced to a barnyard animal at a pageant. A chicken suit.

CHICKEN TWO: I'm just glad to be alive! What about that? You have no survival mechanism! You think the world is safe? Doesn't this prove that it isn't? That an actor of your caliber is reduced to playing a chicken? You think there's respect? You think they—you actually believed that because you had talent they'd spare you!

(*They make chicken noises—clucks and pecks*)

CHICKEN ONE: I'm at the point where I'd rather die. You're right; I never did Hamlet. I never did *Enemy of the People*, I never did Lorca, Marlowe, I never did any of it. No, I never did it. Right. (*Beat*) Oh, it's fine to be a fucking chicken, could've been worse, they might've offered me the part of the—

CHICKEN TWO (*Cuts him off impatiently*): At least you get unemployment benefits because of this job! You won't starve!

CHICKEN ONE (*Agonized, heartbroken*): What good does that do me now? I have no self-respect!

CHICKEN TWO (*Trying not to panic*): If you continue to yell, Michael, then the stage manager will alert the director and someone will come and then something . . . *awful* will happen. Just *awful*. Look at the bright side. Connect to the . . . chicken inside of you. Think of it as an exercise.

(*They cluck and bock*)

CHICKEN ONE: I can't stand this ignominy any longer! I simply won't tolerate it!

CHICKEN TWO (*Holds Chicken One to the ground*): Jesus Michael I beg of you don't get us killed! Please. Please. (*Holds his hand over Michael's mouth—or beak*) Please why can't you be far-sighted? Think of a day when this'll be a laugh? There are people here who have to play pigs, they're lying in pig shit, for ten days! The chicken is a good job. It's a *sign* from them that we'll be rehabilitated. Chicken is harmless. A coward. Let them. Let them think we're cowards. I love you. I don't care that they have reduced us to this, I don't care about the theatre we wanted, I care about you! I love you.

CHICKEN ONE (*After a moment*): Look at us. Two bent chickens at a country fair. There is nothing comic about it. Nothing.

CHICKEN TWO: Look. At least people are laughing. That's something.

CHICKEN ONE: They're laughing, you prick, because they're watching a grown man, an *actor*, in a chicken suit, a *molting* chicken suit for God's sake, hop about in a fucking *coop*! I'd laugh too if it wasn't *me!*

CHICKEN TWO: No, Michael, they're laughing because they appreciate our essaying of a chicken; they laugh because they are delighted.

CHICKEN ONE: Are you fuckin' nuts? Are you kiddin' me? What do you think you *are*? This audience? This is Ice Capades! This is Holiday on Ice! This is your audience! They're laughing because they smell your humiliation, you positively reek of it! "Essaying of a chicken." Please! Don't . . . make . . . me laugh!

(*Pause. Chicken Two hops away*)

CHICKEN TWO: Why can't I be allowed to believe in myself?

CHICKEN ONE: What do you think? You think you're making a statement? You think you're saying something? What exactly do you think you're saying to them?

CHICKEN TWO (*Calm, noble*): If . . . they are aware of who we are, actors, we have been brought . . . low, and yet, who can endow this chore with some semblance of seriousness—some—you know—sense of . . . pride—then they know we have not been destroyed, they know we are not complicit. There.

CHICKEN ONE: If you believe that horseshit, you're an asshole.

CHICKEN TWO (*Simple, direct. Straight*): Michael. Why are you so mean to me?

CHICKEN ONE: Oh, come on.

CHICKEN TWO: No, I mean, this'll be over soon. All of it. You know? Can't you find it in you to be a little bit solicitous, you know, tender? I mean, fuck, I feel bad too. You think I don't know I'm lying to myself? My parents sent me to acting school. My parents came to my plays. My parents loved me, they never dreamt of this kind of treatment for me, and they—they knew everything about me—every boy I—they didn't care—they loved me, they taught me love. And I love you, and I won't be made to feel silly or ridiculous just because I've been forced to wear a fucking chicken suit and humiliate myself for some rubes. This is not humiliation. Humiliation is forgetting how to love, how to love . . . I'd rather die than that . . . and they can put me in a turtle suit, Michael, and shit on me and laugh at me because I amuse them as a queer pansy or a lefty or whore or a hooker or whatever they say, but Michael, you know, it's only a suit. It's only a suit. It's only a suit.

(*Michael says nothing. They bock*)

MICHAEL: I love you too, Terry. I love you too.

(*A man walks onstage. He carries a pointer*)

MAN: These are chickens. They make up a large part of the barnyard world, and they give us eggs, and we eat them and they provide a source of protein for all. The chicken, my friends, she is a truly multifaceted addition to our world. (*Takes out a knife and quickly cuts Chicken Two's throat*) And a friend to mankind at the Nation's table. (*Exits*)
MICHAEL: Bock-bock. Cheep-cheep.

(*He holds the dying Terry in his arms as lights fade down*)

IT CHANGES
EVERY YEAR

First produced at Naked Angels in New York City in February 1993. Nicholas Martin directed the following cast:

Sonia..Angela Thornton
Delia ....Kelly Bishop
Cameron..Geoff Nauffts
Mark...T. Scott Cunningham

Two, small, round cafe tables in two separate restaurants, which is something
we need not realize at first. At both tables, there sits a young man with a
woman of late middle-age. A rainy lunchtime, and the floor is littered with
the accoutrements of that kind of weather; wet macs and umbrellas. Both
tables are some way through bottles of wine. A red for Sonia and Mark, a
white for Cameron and Delia.

TABLE ONE

DELIA: This is so nice, you never think days like this can be any
fun.

CAMERON: I know, I know. With those—awful cards? Hallmark
with like a cat, or a—I don't know, a—worse, a kitten and a
hen and "have a happy Mother's Day." It's so embarrassing.

DELIA: This is much more civilized than getting a card, I think.
This kind of quiet, peaceful, unhurried decent lunch. (Beat) If
only we could get the damn waitress.

TABLE TWO

SONIA: I wonder why we—why I don't get into the city more often.

MARK: We do too, I mean, it's not like you live in Cleveland or something.

SONIA: I always have this argument with Brian, very friendly, but still the man—you know what he's like. "It smells, the rats, the beggars, the traffic . . . "

MARK: Well he's right. Nobody will argue, but still, I mean. Y'know?

SONIA: Well I like that I got to come in like this, without him being so husbandly and—well, you know what he's like! You've seen the—city makes him tense.

MARK: Well, sort of, I guess, I mean he—I don't know what he's thinking so . . .

SONIA (*Cuts him off, comic dismissal*): —Oh he's fine! You know, it's that world, money, work, client, blah . . .

MARK: I actually don't know that world, Sonia.

SONIA (*Drinking wine, a momentary haze*): But to see Manhattan from our house, I sit looking across the sound and you can see it, sometimes—well—you know how I feel out there.

MARK: You can always come in and stay over with us. The sofa is really comfortable if you don't make the mistake of pulling it out into a bed.

(*Waitress enters*)

SONIA: Darling! I was waiting for a—w—that escarole, chicory and goat cheese salad . . . ?

WAITRESS: I'm trying to—it's all—it's Mother's Day, it's all backed up in there—I'm sorry—I'll . . . on . . . tables . . .

TABLE ONE

Waitress seems to be looking around for a certain table. She has a bottle of wine on a tray and two glasses.

DELIA (*To waitress*): Could we, those breadsticks, those cheese sticks, are there any?

WAITRESS: No. That was—the restaurant that used to be in this location did that. We don't. We don't do the cheese sticks. We do the olive bread. People ask all the time.

(*She exits. Beat*)

DELIA: Isn't this still Da Umbella? You can't keep up in this town! What were we talkin' about, honey?

(*They drink and smoke while eating*)

CAMERON: Uhh . . . let's see, I was taking exception to your statement that "Children make rotten historians."

DELIA (*Guffaws*): Yeah, that's where we were alright. Boy. You boys are amazing. Well you do, you twist everything around so it suits you. And we can't defend ourselves. The stories that get, you know, twisted around. I'll tell ya.

CAMERON: What's interesting, Delia, about history is—it's usually written by the victors, by the winners, right?

DELIA: I guess. Okay. That's a fair statement, I suppose, if you like, I'll buy that. I love this wine.

CAMERON (*Laughs*): Well, okay, if it is true that children make lousy historians, it's because, you see, we kids, we're the victims, we're not the winners. Children write history for sympathy.

(*Beat*)

DELIA (Smiles): Don't be such a little smarty-pants, Cam. (Beat) So come on, tell me, tell me about Mark, I want to hear about Mark. (Beat) What does he really think of me?

CAMERON: You don't want to know that do you? You do? Do you? He loves you. Loves.

DELIA: I'm having such a nice time! Pour me a little more of that Merlot, will ya, kiddo? It's got such a kick to it, boy-oh-boy. I better not get drunk. (Beat) Get me drunk, will you Cam, I've gotta work tonight and I'd like to just show up once, just once at the hotel and be blotto.

CAMERON: Maybe we should look at the desserts?

DELIA: Not enough that I have booze but then I'll crash from the sugar. Watch me slug some Brit tourist. They're the worst. The Brits. The men. The women just look like they've been screwed over. Ohh. Listen to me. Yes. Let's have dessert.

(Waitress comes in again, looking more and more undone. She is loaded down with glasses)

TABLE TWO

SONIA: So we came in to go to some play with music that some son of some client of Brian's composed the music for, we bundled into their Volvo and then up into some dank thing of a theatre up some bad stairs . . .

MARK: We got the waitress!

SONIA: Sweetie, we ordered a Kahlua bread pudding with hard sauce and a Harvey Wallbanger cake and . . .

MARK (Frantic): Since you're here why not add two grappas? Two grappas, okay? Just two grappas?

WAITRESS (Runs off): I'll try, I don't know what they've got left back there!

SONIA: Anyhow. This theatre we went to, you know, some untalented son of some client of my third husband's written the music, which is really, just a long sort of atonal complaint really, complaining in public about his childhood; a long, headachy, atonal complaint, all done with this sort of very accusatory atonal twang.

MARK: You were on Twenty-third Street?

SONIA (*Nods, drinks, smokes*): We couldn't come by or anything. We had these people with us.

MARK: No. That's okay.

SONIA: A block away from you and Cameron. I would have liked to. I was sitting there with the headache music in my head, just wanting to slip off and come over to you boys. I should've.

MARK: That would've been nice.

SONIA: Why is it so much art is about how awful we parents were?

MARK: Oh, like *all* art? Uh-huh, I mean, that's sort of a *broad*, don't you think, statement—

SONIA: I mean tell me the truth. Did you have such an *awful* childhood? (*Beat*) Was it that bad? (*Beat*) You kids. You won't even answer me? I'm not dangerous, you know *that*. Like an honest talk. So one can understand. Better. Where we are today.

MARK: Oh no, let's not do this, this isn't, it's Mother's Day, let's not do that. I just know that this place used to be a laundromat. Maybe they still do it for all I know. Fluff and fold and frittata while you wait.

SONIA: Ah. The boundaries. The boundaries you children put up. Brian bought, you know, you haven't been out since Brian got this "Invisible Fence" for the dogs. They get a shock if they start to run off the property line. You know they *want* to run away. These dogs. They would if they *could*. (*Beat*) One thinks of one's child when the Jack Russells get a shock a few acres away as they try and escape. One thinks of one's kids.

(*Mark smiles at this. Sonia does too*)

What? What is it?

MARK: You're funny, is all. That's all

SONIA: Yes, well, quite. Yes. You didn't know that about me? As I've always told my children, "Without a sense of humor, one is simply another statistic."

MARK: Yeah, I've heard it before. Many times. Many times. But let me tell you, Sonia, in my experience knowing how to fight is just as valuable.

SONIA: Oh but sweetheart, they go hand in hand don't they? You didn't like your fish, did you?

(The waitress appears with a tray laden with dirty dishes. She looks around, undone, as everyone, Sonia and Mark, Cameron and Delia, gestures for her attention. The tray wobbles and almost falls. A single plate crashes to the floor. Delia and Cameron react, startled. Mark and Sonia do not)

TABLE ONE

DELIA: What I'm trying to understand here, the thing that's good about this lunch is, I'd like to understand, you know, the grudge. Where's it come from? You think things are goin' so damn good and suddenly there's this—well it gets chilly, and I'm thinking "Hey, I'm his mom, what'd I do wrong?"

(There is a moment while Cameron drinks)

CAMERON: Mark and I recently had a very severe fight and I yelled in a way I had never yelled before, it seems. And I threw a glass, which broke on the floor. And he started sobbing. And I left. And he didn't come back for hours. And was still sobbing when he did. I apologized and held him. But he kept saying the same thing over and over. *(Beat)* Like a small child. He said "You scare me, you *scare me*, you scare me."

DELIA: Uh-huh. Yeah. Uh-huh. Right. So?

CAMERON: Eventually when it had quieted down, it turned into a talk about mothers. We each had responded to childhood stimuli. Mothers. You bring them with you, always, see? And so that gets hard.

DELIA: Oy with the blaming of the mothers. Oy with the history business, I'm just a woman workin' in a hotel, oy with the "bringing." What're you telling me?

CAMERON: Well. Mark said "My mother. Something happened. When you yelled. My mother." Something awful happened . . .

DELIA: It's now my fault that you have a temper? (*Beat. She drinks*) Shit. Spare me. Spare mothers the memories of their sons.

(*The waitress returns shaking her head*)

CAMERON: I was thinking we could get maybe a couple of desserts? A tiramisu a . . .

DELIA: The creme caramel, hon, without the goo—

CAMERON: And two lattes. . . . Why do you keep shaking your head like that?

WAITRESS: We're out.

DELIA: Of which?

WAITRESS: Of everything. They didn't make enough. There's no more dessert.

CAMERON (*Panic*): Not even some biscotti? The little amaretto? Ones? With the . . .? You know? The *round*?

WAITRESS: There's nothing left. There's one order of broccoli rabe that table three sent back and I think, like some, French chamomile tea.

DELIA: (*Heartbroken*): Something sweet would be so nice right now . . .

(*The waitress looks at her with sympathy and reaches into her apron pocket and takes out a Three Musketeers bar and puts it on the table*)

WAITRESS: Happy Mother's Day. (*Exits*)

DELIA: It's not fair to blame us for it all!

CAMERON (*Quiet*): Yes. It isn't. But that's what we do, isn't it?

Sons. And mothers. I have only *one* friend, and I have a lot of friends, but only *one* who loves, loves, loves beyond compare his mother, and they're friends. And you know what she gave him? (*Beat*) A lion's courage, but most of us, we get fear and—no—no you *give us* fear. And where does that leave us? So we *do* blame you, and we blame you for all of it, every slight, every fuck-up, every bad day, we've got to fight it forever. And I'm sorry. It's childish and sad and pathetic for all of us. Sons and mothers. And I don't have any answers for you.

DELIA: Well. Boy, I thought this might be different.

CAMERON: I don't think it means that we don't really love you but. . . . It is childish of us, isn't it?

DELIA: I've worked in a hotel for years. Before that, you know, I worked at Tiffany's. Life is so long. So . . . forgive me, Cam, so *fucking* long, sweetie. You know? You guys, I hope you come 'round. In my work, you hold a grudge, you die.

CAMERON: Auden. We must love each other or die.

DELIA: Uh-huh. That's terrific, he must've been really smart. Auden.

TABLE TWO

SONIA: The question is, "Do sons like their mothers?" I look at this restaurant and I can imagine mothers all over town, aching, just *aching* and getting dressed up like I did this morning, and what? Dread? Hey, ohhh. Dread, aching and dreading it, all over this city, all over this country but still, coming to these awful ritual things, and nobody hates rituals as much as me. A restaurant filled with mothers. Being led out.

(*Beat*)

MARK: I'm sorry. I don't know what to say.

SONIA: I am *tired* of all this human business, this day to day human business—where's the *life* in it all? (*Beat*) Oh, God. Look at this. Mothers being taken out to lunch. I wonder how many are being taken out to lunch by their sons' boyfriends?

MARK: Oh, in this town, I'd say it's about seventy percent, Sonia.

SONIA (*Smiles*): Cam can't joke with me about these things. But you can. Oh well.

WAITRESS (*To Sonia and Mark*): This is a Drambuie cookie, no one else wants it. But it might help. It's supposed to be sort of good.

MARK: Then why don't you have it?

WAITRESS: I'm allergic.

TABLE ONE

Delia gets up and puts on her raincoat. Cameron watches her. She rustles about in her bag and extracts something wrapped.

DELIA: Listen, Cam, this is, will you give this to Mark for me? A cup he liked that I have. I actually lifted it from Tiffany's when I worked there. (*Beat*) I thought I'd have to hock it to buy us food, that's how little those shits paid us back then. He loved the fact that I couldn't, just couldn't get rid of it. Unsentimental value, huh? Unsentimental value, right? Listen, Cam. Thanks for lunch, hon. I better get outta here. The men get all the cabs when it rains in this town. You have to fight like one of those little red chinese soldiers just to get a goddamn taxi in this town.

(*Cameron gets up and kisses her*)

CAMERON: Bye Dee.

DELIA: Listen, hon. You said something about history: Let me tell you about history. Here's what happened. I had a son. It's that simple. And here's a message. Tell him that the two of you are invited for dinner most nights.

(*Delia exits. Cameron watches her go and sits down at the table*)

TABLE TWO

Sonia rises. She takes out a little package wrapped in red tissue paper. it jingles metallically.

SONIA: Will you give this to Cam, please? They're cufflinks from his father.

MARK: The real one?

SONIA: My second and third husbands were just men. Not fathers. The one who died. Yes. I always kept them, held onto them, because they never lost the man's smell and in all my subsequent marriages, whenever there was a bad day, and there have been many, I would go to them and jiggle them, just jiggle them around. Smell him. And take some strength out of it. (*Beat*) Cameron loved him so much. I thought he would like these. I thought that at this stage, they might mean something. More. To him. Than to me.

(*She holds his hand in hers, giving him the package. Mark says nothing, nodding*)

Well. I would have liked to have seen my son. Today. On Mother's Day.

MARK: I thought you didn't like rituals.

SONIA: I don't. But I do rather like my son.

MARK: He likes you, Sonia.

SONIA: Actually, I suspect that he does. Thank you for lunch,

Mark. It has certainly been the most unusual Mother's Day of my many years of having children do odd things.

(Sonia puts on her rain gear and exits. The waitress comes to Mark with the bill)

WAITRESS: I'm sorry about all the dessert problems, we took it off the bill.
MARK *(Dry)*: Gee. Thanks.
WAITRESS: Mother's Day, Father's Day, Valentine's Day, you should know, a tip, don't bother going out. It's hell. I didn't even know it was Mother's Day today because it changes every year and so you can't—anyway, it's a bad day to show up for work.
CAMERON *(Signs check)*: Aren't they all, honey?

(Waitress exits. Mark sits down next to Cameron)

How was it?
MARK: She gave me something for you.
CAMERON: Oh. Yours did too!

(They exchange packages and start unwrapping)

MARK *(Unwrapping)*: Isn't that sweet?
CAMERON *(Tearing the paper)*: Isn't that funny? . . . Oh.

(They are both silent as they come upon the gifts. A moment of recognition. Each holds his present as the lights fade)

Recipe for One,

or

A Handbook for Travelers

First produced at Circle Repertory Company, New York City, Tanya Berezin, Artistic Producer, in March 1994. Ray Cochran directed Zeljko Ivanek.

A very dashing young man in black tie sits in an overstuffed armchair. Perhaps the stuffing, on closer examination, is coming out. Chilling next to him is a bottle of champagne. He holds a flute glass, and drinks and smokes without relent, as much as possible. Also beside him, on a small stand, is a clear glass bowl filled to the top with caviar. He dips his hand and licks the shiny black eggs off at will.

Recently, I remembered Schwab's pharmacy. It was next to the old Garden of Allah. This is the old Sunset Boulevard. The Garden of Allah, of course, was where Chaplin and Fitzgerald and Groucho and Fatty and Dietrich would go to drink and fuck wildly by the pool.

(Beat)

All dead now, as is Schwab's and the Garden of Allah itself. Which was torn down in that "I've got a marvelous idea, let's tear down this great thing and put up a strip mall" manner that has become the fashion.

(Beat)

Sometimes I think I've seen far too much beauty destroyed.
In any case, Schwab's had an extremely famous chocolate ice
cream soda.

(*He wanders about the stage, remembering, smoking, and drinking and eating excitedly throughout giving the recipe*)

Two tablespoons of chocolate syrup, one of milk, one large
scoop chocolate ice cream, all placed in the bottom of a ten-
ounce glass; stir well while gently filling the glass with the
carbonated water. Stir gently . . . into the night.

(*He stops sadly*)

Serves one. Serves only one. . . . I used to sit at that counter
and think about luck. Mythology has it that Lana Turner was
discovered at that counter. Such absurdly precise luck, that,
the miracle of being in exactly the right place at the right
time. I have had my own share of good luck.

(*He smokes again, and then coughs horribly for a long moment. He catches
his breath and thinks*)

There is a marvelous Noel Coward song called "Let's Live
Dangerously." From a thirties show of his called *Words and
Music*. I . . . remember the opening night. Everyone was there.
The Sitwells, the Woolfs, Binky. Noel himself, Shaw. G.B.
Shaw to one side of me. Amazing night. Amazing nights there
used to be. In any case, the second refrain of that song went
straight into my heart, just the way *La Forza del Destina* did that
first night at La Scala and Balanchine's . . . Paris with
Diaghalev? I . . .

(*He shakes his head, lost in memory. Coughs*)

That is another story. But the second refrain of "Let's Live Dangerously" . . .

(*He sings with a growing-exhausted, weary Torch bitterness*)

> Let's live dangerously dangerously dangerously,
> Let's grab every opportunity we can,
> Let's swill
> Each pill
> Destiny has in store,
> Absorbing life at every pore
> We'll scream and yell for more.
> Let's live turbulently turbulently turbulently,
> Let's add something to the history of man,
> Come what may
> We'll be spectacular
> And say, "Hey! Hey!"
> In the vernacular,
> And so until we break beneath the strain
> In various ways
> We're going to be raising Cain.

(*He shakes his head, lost in some memory. He sways, dancing to some music only he can hear*)

I think that is a terribly happy song. I used to hum it at all those lucky places. The counter at Schwab's. The bar at Trader Vic's. The basement at Studio . . . Regine's. The old Harry's Bar. I— One has watched so many of the lucky places one used to go to just disappear until you look around and you're in this . . . Diaspora of the present.

(*He pours more champagne, runs his fingers through his hair. He coughs, and drinks, and takes some pills out of his pocket. He unties his tie*)

Fuck. When I—when I *heard* that song, there was a sensation of something molecular within me unraveling and then the DNA coming back together again differently, and sitting there, I felt such a flash of recognition. Myself. One sometimes feels that as a sort of elixir. A sort of heat. The sort of heat we only know when we fuck.

God, I do love those words, "When we fuck." What else is there? Now, however, it's—it's . . . *food* that's the acceptable alternative. (In New York City I discovered recently a television channel where at night all they do is fuck, but it seems that the channel where all they do is *cook* is far more popular.) But I think . . . that before there was pesto, there was the great thrust of two bodies entwined and lost in a kind of grace . . .

(*Beat*)

I am planning a perfect party, a kind of ongoing happening, the kind we used to have. . . . There are so many things to do. We start with . . .

(*A hacking cough. He shakes his head*)

. . . Miami to South Beach to watch the models. Which I used to do in the old days in Paris before everything changed . . . *again.* . . . Then to New Orleans, to drink in the streets and listen to the Preservation Hall band and all that music for the dead . . . all that music for the dead.

(*Beat. Drinks*)

Some will be tired, I expect. At this point. But for those who are not, ah, across the pond on the Normandy or the—across the Atlantic for a . . .

(*He stops, trying to remember what they'll do*)

Oh. I must add sex to the list. Sex. When I say sex it is the kind they don't know anymore, the kind we used to have in the old days, that . . . shock of a body. The cold water shock of a fuck. Without, of course, rules. Rules.

I suppose some of my friends will be tired, and need to rest.

(*He coughs. He then rather tiredly puts his finger in the caviar and stirs slowly. He looks at his black finger. Shakes his head in awe*)

This stuff is so very very good. They say—they say—they say you can't actually taste it after the first popping explosion of brine on the tongue, that the taste buds are simply dulled by the salt. I say, quite simply, that is a lie. For it is, you see, the salt one remembers, the salt of a kiss you are remembering . . .

(*He hesitates, bringing his finger to his mouth; then, instead of eating, he wipes his finger off with a white pocket square*)

I haven't thought about Paris. We go to Paris. For the second act of this party. And we move Southward, after the duck at Tour D'Argent, we go to that place Josephine Baker used to dance at. . . . . She's gone too.

(*He takes, from his pocket, an old and terribly worn Baedeker guidebook. Pages fall out and onto the floor. He looks sad, shakes his head at this*)

This volume was new, of course, when I got it. They don't think of making these things to last. A book should be like a cathedral. The rot that afflicts a book, it is the second worst kind of decay I see. You can never finish anything. When I think of the first editions I've lost. *Remembrance of Things Past. Vanity Fair.*

(*Beat. A whisper*)

That Oscar Wilde . . . I . . . they all turn to dust and acid powder in one's hands. I had, for many years, a particular drawing in my possession. Of a machine for making ice. Da Vinci. Lost. The only one.

(*He looks at the book*)

Oh dear. In any case. I have planned the next act of this marvelous party . . . from *The Mediterranean, Seaports and Sea Routes. A Handbook for Travelers*, by Karl Baedeker, nineteen eleven. There is a lovely route in it, Constantinople to Odessa. And Dubrovnik, which one hears is no longer not so lovely. But we could . . . look from the boat. If all the guests are too tired, I suppose I could wait. Yes. There is a lovely prayer in the *Handbook for Travelers*. . . .

(*He opens the book, and tries to catch the light, squinting. He takes out a pair of half-glasses and peers at the page*)

Sometimes my eyes. Hmn. Here it is:

> Go little book, God send thee good passage,
> And specially let this be thy prayere
> Unto them all that thee will read or hear:
> Where thou art wrong, after their help to call,
> Thee to correct in any part or all.

(*He closes the book. He lights another cigarette*)

There is so much we of this party have to look forward to. Paris. Paris? I wonder what they'll be wearing in Paris after they tear down the Eiffel Tower and the Louvre. Probably something I can't even *imagine*.

(*Beat*)

Did I mention that it seems to me that I am the luckiest boy in the world? And that I'm going to live forever . . . ? The kind of luck that makes you laugh forever? Literally. You laugh forever when you have my particular brand of Lana Turner luck.

Lana Turner, of course, it turns out, never really even went to Schwab's drugstore for a chocolate ice cream soda. But it does make for a nice story. Doesn't it?

(*The lights begin to fade*)

Maybe a nap would be nice before the party continues? Sleep. Ah, sleep. It's such a pleasure. It's almost a sort of fucking, don't you think?

(*Beat*)

Sleep?

(*The lights go down as he lights another smoke, and he is illuminated for a moment by the matchlight—a tired and haggard young face—and then blows out the match, leaving us with only a glowing red ember in dark space*)